THE UNVEILING

poems by

Perry S. Nicholas

Finishing Line Press
Georgetown, Kentucky

THE UNVEILING

For Ronan and Mali from Papou

ACKNOWLEDGMENTS

The poems Polyxeni and Two Roads both appeared in *Just Poets Anthology*,
2022 and 2023.

Publisher: Leah Huete de Maines
Editor: Christen Kincaid
Cover Art:Photo by jag_cz
Author Photo: Perry S. Nicholas
Cover Design: Elizabeth Maines McCleavy

Order online: www.finishinglinepress.com
also available on amazon.com

Author inquiries and mail orders:
Finishing Line Press
PO Box 1626
Georgetown, Kentucky 40324
USA

Table of Contents

1.

ISLAND WALK

I wish on the island of your heart
you allow me to walk the perimeter,
be the lee shore, the shelter
your eyes strain to find through fog.
A test of its boundaries
across a one-mile radius,
our journey might still feel infinite.
I'll meet your vessel, delicately
gather what treasures I can carry to you,
bring them to the untouched edge of the sea.

I STAND, QUIETLY

I stand, quietly, witness
you crossing the footbridge
in the old park where almost no one
dares walk alone anymore.

Life on the outskirts is dark,
we fear walking on our own—
defenseless, unsure of purpose.
To love, lust, or just to be?

I stand, softly, whisper words
only swaying trees share,
birds pass over—squirrels trample
my simple outlook now.

In this moment, standing quietly,
detecting how the world's breath
labors to return to full blown,
I pray I can keep my balance.

I no longer question if I've found my focus.
I just choose not to follow you further.
A different world—the park seems smaller now.
I stand quietly, and quietly, I stand out.

WAKE

I must admit I feel some guilt,
albeit tiny, at not attending your mother's wake,
but I knew you'd be there in full strut
with your crazy-as a-shithouse-rat brother,
who misunderstood the approach she took
to life long after losing her natural beauty,
still believing she looked like Ann-Margaret
in her prime, mini-skirt and all, shimmying
around a sneering Elvis and flipping her hair.

If she could lift her head up once more,
would she smile as if coming on to the King?
I like to think she would enjoy it,
that is, me poeticizing her early image,
trying to pass along some of the wisdom
of age I have acquired to you, especially
during these last years you wished me dead, too.
She might appreciate the effort, heartfelt
and full of strain as it was. Maybe if I explain

I came to flatter her hairdo and not to see
if her wooden coffin was any more comfortable
than her rented nursing home bed,
she might welcome the truth of that gesture.
She wouldn't expect me to hug or kiss her,
as I never did in life, but realize I understood
her coy flirting, feigned hard-of-hearing,
Clinique eyeliner, which all might guilt you
into leaning over her body one final time.

I'M SORRY

For A Poet Friend Under a Waxing Crescent Moon

I'm sorry if the first thing I do
is reach for a pen to scribble,

after pouring an ouzo to soothe
my throat, read a perfect phrase

of yours, my then-alive friend,
who shouldn't have died

except for this fucking virus
nobody expected or understands,

your only weakness you could not
protect yourself and more simply—

you got old. It wasn't your fault.
Sorry if I seem a little touchy,

but the night is peaceful here with poetry,
crickets, and the absence of touch.

Forgive me. I'm alone, the hunter's moon
houses your voice, and I'm still writing.

NEW NORMAL

I still argue with you in my sleep
about everything from tv, music,

money, to friends and love.
We never finish, but I know how it ends.

I'd give anything to create less noise.
Anything to break apart old thoughts.

Every time I dream, I die more,
a little closer to darkness

than truth, but better than those
constant awakenings in the night,

ones I mastered during my longest year.
Some words I can make out, others I can't:

*What did you say? That's not what
I meant. Can we just start over?*

These days, I've accepted a new normal:
I relish arguing with you, all night, in my sleep.

THE UNVEILING

When the time comes,
Will we want to take off our masks?
—Poet Rachel Hadas

I'm not ready to remove mine.
I like that you have to work hard

to understand my tone, read my eyes,
wonder if we should hug,

question if our hands should touch,
continue along the path of not-quite-knowing

which side of the wall we stand,
or whether we will ever join forces.

When the veil lifts and we're all the same,
I won't be able to discern how strong

you were during the immoral reign
of a maskless face peering out of Pandora's box.

It makes me believe maybe I don't need anyone
to make me mindful and mouthless.

These days, I still dream you wearing a disguise,
dark eyes squinting, air-kissing my cheeks.

2.

IN YOUR POCKET

I go back to writing this down
on a yellow legal pad,

the simple method we used
to share ideas in years past,

back and forth across right-handed
desks, two out-of-place lefties.

Do you have something to write with?
You take the next two lines.

Maybe if we had a little more time,
we would have actually finished our poem,

begun the transformation, editing,
necessary to move to press and save.

You could find a poem in your pocket,
stin tsépi sas, as the old Greeks used to say.

And I have wasted so many turns by over-thinking.
Now, you're up again, but you don't answer,

since you decided to pass on, so I
have to decide everything: topic, title, even

if writing it down is worthwhile at all.
As for me, old friend,

 I suppose I'll keep on trying.
But you, you bring the pencil.

POLYXENI (Είναι όλα ελληνικά για μένα)

I remember your father cursing you
in the overcrowded shack to *stop
parading around in your nightgown
in front of your young cousin, like a putana.*

It was always Greek to us.
You stormed out, proud and defiant in lace—
to punish you, he beat our grandmother.
I didn't have the balls to beat him back.

Young girl with porcelain skin,
bright, ceramic shine, like Aegean stars!
Where could you go but up and away,
escape those memories on the earth below?

The last time I saw you,
hair transformed to moon-white,
you wore the same defiant look
as you described your condition,

the cancer waning you to non-existence.
You still seemed illumined to me.
Did you relive that scene 50 years before?
Did I capture your phase here accurately?

Dear, I think you must have buried it deep,
like shells in the sand on the island *paralia*,
along with brightness, a delicate nightgown,
and the poor bones of our blackened *yiayia*.

TWO ROADS

I shall be telling this with a sigh
Somewhere ages and ages hence
—Robert Frost

Only English outside our home,
my father would warn as we left
for our American school, already afraid
that we, little foreign boys
whose mother talked funny,
would be singled out as different,
dumber than our classmates.

We call you Perry, not Pantelis,
because it sounds less foreign,
likely after the crooner-of-the-decade Como;
they crossed out the Greek on my birth certificate.
My baptism in American waters scared me
from wandering too far in either direction,
so I chose a path of shy and smart.

Books and silence and more books,
working to be more than a two-headed
student of life and language.
I waded deeper into the woods of my education,
only to return home, feel guilt at those left behind.
Parents long gone before I veered toward this fork—
writing, speaking, reading, translating, and I—

I took what appeared to be the sensible road—
but what difference did it really make?
Now, not sorry I learned to travel both,
navigate the middle with balance and grace.

ATHENS AT CHRISTMAS

Cheeks already half full of Campari,
we couldn't help but laugh as we fed
each other roasted chestnuts, huddled up
under strings of lights, close to outdoor heaters.

I still taste cherry on your lips.
You sip it on the rocks, no soda,
squint over my shoulder at the Parthenon,
right there above Syntagma Square, hovering

in a winter sky with Athena waiting for us
to disengage and ascend, depart
the most wide-awake place in our world,
epicenter of the polis, *Parayiorgos Café.*

Χριστούγεννα στην Αθήνα, once my reprieve,
where even a warrior goddess wouldn't leave.

LE PREVISIONI DEL TEMPO (WEATHER REPORT)

Today, *il tempo non bello,*
lacking emotion and sunlight,
loveliness and love.

I choose to sit alone
on a cold stone bench
like a dog waiting

for the next car to race by,
changing the landscape a bit,
alter my forecast of thought
and ask: *Che tempo fa?*

Nothing changes, just a slight wind.
Clouds grow darker, *piu scuro*—
threatening, yet non-committal.

I observe this day in reverse—
truly believe in transformation, then
adjust my pace in step with *il cielo sereno.*

And after I conjure a cleansing rain,
this world no longer seems so
parched, weak, and trivial.

Sta sera, it feels wet, more spirited, and full.

FLOATERS

Cara, ho semplicemente sognato noi?

Chasing after shadows
of everything we shared,
those moments dart away—

like following floaters,
unsure glances to either side,
detached specks of time.

A web of memories,
snarled in a netting,
upon wakening I wonder:

Cara, did I merely dream us,
somewhere in a far corner
of my mind's eye?

3.

I STAND IN FRONT OF THE DAKOTA

with Lennon, Frost, and Cummings

Someone once labelled me a *lost soul*, too.
Standing here, I wonder about certain things:

why we have no privacy,
project ourselves up on a screen

bored people feel entitled
to watch for free entertainment.

No one loves themselves enough, so they
stalk, uncover, mold what they need.

I walk alone, you're gone, your family
dispersed, broken pieces of hurt

floating around the world like musical notes.
Now am I free to be poetical?

A Gothic brick façade: gated,
narrow entranceway, no sign,

flowered tenderness, your lined face.
A folded, tossed away story of a lunatic.

And a *beautiful, beautiful,*
beautiful, beautiful boy.

Now *here is the bud of the bud:*
I wait, wonder if you were ever

free to cross into Central Park alone,
like I do today, listening for your footsteps.

MOUTHING THE WORDS

You're gonna make me give myself a good talking to
—Bob Dylan

I'm sometimes curious if people
who pass me on my morning walk
wonder just what it is
I am talking to myself about.

Do they try to read my lips,
decipher my words, usually
arranged in poetic lines,
matching the rhythm of my stride?

Frost counts his horse's pace in the snow.
Auden mimics a death march knell.
But sometimes a walk is just a walk,
mumbles connecting isolated steps.

Whatever pace, whatever message
my damaged voice box may squeak,
I don't really care how much they hear—
I try not to take myself so seriously.

To some, I'm sure, it appears to be a rant,
to others I must be singing a song.
So subjective the theme of this poetry,
however observers interpret my mouthing.

VAN GOGH AFTER THE PANDEMIC

A colorist I am not,
even though my methods
have changed, landscape shifted
a touch beyond these faded images.

I leaf through old photographs,
ones depicting us as sowers,
king and queen of the wheatfield—
making love, jealous, every stroke in between.

I am not a colorist,
but my hues have brightened some—
more yellows, more effort to capture
space between your eyelashes,

ask questions we never dared answer,
simplify, fill in all our pencil lines.
I have lived alone so long
inside blacks and whites,

there is no choice but to bandage
wounds, pursue color in a flurry,
create thicker, longer brushstrokes of apology.
I'm nothing greater than my last self-portrait.

I wonder if he might have added more crows.
I wonder if this is my last attempt, too.
You, the unabashed auctioneer, and this,
my humble, colorless offering.

HOW MUCH TIME (HAVE I WASTED SEEKING PERFECTION)?

Inspired by a line by Julie Danho

Loss of time and loss of love.
Now we meet at this marker,

a place we fear may not matter.
How much hard work lies beyond?

We may reach and stretch forever:
is this the couplet we strive for?

They were beautiful in life,
and in death they were not divided.

Eating for the sake of eating,
kissing by instinct and searching.

Is it wasted, this life of constant typing,
still walking the night, fingers cramped?

I don't care to live in your everyday world.
Dear, accept these years, my imperfect gift.

SHELF LIFE

On my 69th birthday

When I finally let go,
memories of me will have
a shelf life of three days:

the first for all to rest up
from watching and waiting,
second for sifting through

signed books, the third,
for the moon to appear with no
exclamation on my end.

The quiet will close quickly,
dark around the language of light—
nothing will ever change.

Read a poem for me after searching
stocked cupboards, raid my computer
for passwords to secret prizes.

A poet once said romantic love
has a half-life of two years
before it spoils forever.

He probably had the timing right,
left preserves in the pantry too long,
and I too will likely topple while reaching.

ABOVE THE CITY

I stand on a 10th floor balcony next to you,
in a scattered frame of mind,
as people move in and out of restaurants,
grocery stores, infinite bars of beer—
high above where everything moves
and surrounds us, where we search
for words on billboards, buses, bookstores,
full phrases that might stimulate, unite.

I've no idea what you are about to do—
take a swan dive as your swan song—
and maybe you don't either at that point,
but here, high above our city of pain,
a leap is inevitable, at least that's how
your choice seems to me. I'll go back,
re-visit your thick volume of poems
for clues, a broken lifeline of stories.

I guess I never imagined you would
go through with it, draw in your wings
as you cannonball through the air,
where written in the sky are lines
of poetry, scribbled and alive—
Dylan Thomas and Hart Crane mostly—
we haven't yet finished our poetic class.

Maybe you're floating after Thomas and Crane.
I'll remain here, for now, on this side of the rail.

4.

THE POETRY SCENE

Do we have time for one or two more?
I've waited so long through all the others.
I don't really care, would be out the door
except I need to read one for my mother.

My poem's the best, the rest are not smart,
of any concern to my craft, my friends.
It's not about you, it's not about art—
I write to find out whose ear I can bend.

The one I just wrote on my way over here
is ten pages long and will change the world.
It will touch your heart and conjure a tear,
and may even help me impress some girl.

Sit back and listen, I'm sure you'll agree—
it's all about me, me, me, me, and me.

PALMER METHOD

Inspired by a Ken Feltges poem

Leaning forward in our seats,
wrapped around right-handed desks,
we smudged our hands in our own ink,
trying so hard to create ovals
like all the acceptable kids
who were born slanted to the right.
We lefties were the oddballs,
struggling for acceptance
from our peers and teachers,
afraid to unleash demons

that might lurk inside, end up
on the wrong side of God,
or even worse, to be left behind.
It was hard enough I was looked at
as a foreigner with a mother who
talked funny, a house that always
smelled of grease, full of people who lived
in two very split worlds, judged
by the majority in their right minds.

So I learned to create silly circles,
at least look as if I was concentrating,
waited for times to change, outlooks
to bend back the other way, people
to accept us as special scriveners
who could use both hands equally,
prove to them left is just unique,
and really, all is right with our world.

THE EPIPHANY, THE BOND, AND THE MOON

Time to settle all our remaining rifts,
forgive and forget should be the true goal.
Twelve days travelling, they brought the gifts,
though this year nothing but a lump of coal.

I dove for the cross when I was a boy,
swam to the bottom and searched for old gold.
The sea and the stars became my real toys
until I learned we can't help but grow old.

Pen and dictionary took up their space,
gilded ladies galore painted their bond
on my heart, my wallet, my courting case—
this all left me with a need to respond:

rather than failing to forget and forgive,
accept this moon as the right place to live.

GOOD LEASHES

Something there is that doesn't love a leash,
perhaps a test to show you don't need me.
I work hard to restrain this yelping beast
who'd rather find a good length to feel free.

On the one hand, we struggle to stay close,
the other, we need to find our own way.
You sniff at me with your Cyrano nose
while I pull and guide you every day.

What is the true answer to this riddle?
I say *elves*, you say *what?*
We divide our life right down the middle,
God says do what you want to but...

You tug hard: *Don't do me any favors.*
I let loose: *Good leashes make good neighbors.*

NO KNOWN EXPLANATION

the voice of your eyes is deeper than all roses
—e.e.cummings

I've grown tired of explaining sonnets,
how they alternate rhyme, force themselves
into meter, search for a turn that doesn't
sound so contrived, but still sings true.

Let me say it this way:
I'd rather hold you without words,
explore spaces and silences, fill
tiny crevices we leave out of hesitancy
and flowery getting-to-know-yous.

Lovely is as your loveliness does—
right now, it shames me to admit I'm a writer.
Your eyes take the place of any resolution,
curve of your back tells a deeper story.

We've found what we wish to be in this moment:
a quiet couplet needing no known explanation.

GRAMMAR LESSON

I left behind my life as a teacher,
(can barely teach myself anymore)

but watching you walk your dog
and cat in tandem at 6 am

in your pajama shorts is an advanced lesson
in foreign verse. One of inspiration,

spontaneity, form, and inflection.
I imagine you reading Shelley,

wonder how you might read the line:
"soul meets soul on lovers' lips".

When you pass by me close,
cut through the vulnerable morning,

you share the click of your Russian tongue
as you recite loudly on speaker phone.

It's as if I'm sitting in the back
of a classroom, and you are roaming

between the rows, the teacher
I can't take my eyes off.

Your laughter is your lesson,
a gift not many offer up lately.

Metered slap of your sandals
match my old heart.

It's your attempt to teach me simple grammar,
but baby, I ain't nothin' like Shelley.

DONE THE BUTTONS UP WRONG

A phrase lifted from
a Japanese writer sums up exactly
what may have gone awry

in all the relationships I have fucked up.
Or should I not view it that way, but,
as one suggested, I was not *lovely* enough.

I've noticed more than one woman
in my life has taken to using

just about everything: *lovely* day,
lovely word, *lovely* feelings,
lovely the way you used to touch me.

As you squeeze into your *lovely* bodice,
I fumble to unbutton the back
of your A-line dress, try again and again,

'til we admit we will fail forever.
It's like this: *we simply done the buttons up wrong.*

ONE LAST LOOK

I never fall in love at night...
        —Jack Nicholson in "The Crossing Guard"

There has to be an end to poems
about the moon and death.

What new can be said?
The moon has been compared

to every possible object, and death,
well, leaves you speechless.

Any angle you use to approach it,
measure distance or time,

the best-case scenario is love—
the usual phase just fades.

So make it a point to fall
in love during daylight,

leave the moon to those
who expect nothing, write little,

tire when they strain their eyes upward.

Perry S. Nicholas is a Professor Emeritus of English at SUNY at ERIE in Buffalo, N.Y. where he was awarded the SUNY Chancellor's Award and the President's Outstanding Teacher Award. He has published one textbook of poetry prompts, three full-length and six chapbooks of original poetry, along with two CDs of poetry. You can see his work at *perrynicholas.com*.

His poems have appeared in *Common Ground Review, Literary House Review, Caesura, Word Worth, Silver Birch Press, Snapdragon, Verse-Virtual, Slant, Feile-Festa, Louisiana Literature, Chautauqua Literary Journal, Chest, The Healing Muse, New York Quarterly, Great Lakes Review, Chronogram,* and *AHI*. His poems have also appeared on over twenty occasions in the *Buffalo News*. They also appear in the anthologies *Right Here, Right Now, Resurrection of a Sunflower, Flash in the Dark,* and a *Celebration of Western New York Poets*.

Perry has judged the *Just Buffalo* poetry contest, the New York State *Poetry Out Loud* competition, the *Word Worth* fiction contest, and has been guest lecturer at Villa Maria College, Niagara Community College, Buffalo State College, Medaille College, Daemen College, and New York College in Athens, Greece. He has read his poetry in Plymouth, NYC, Woodstock, Albany, Schenectady, New Paltz, and Saratoga Springs. He has been nominated for the Pushcart Prize on four occasions.

During his recent retirement, he has been interviewed for both Stockbridge, MA Library and the Hellenic American Project for Queens College, NYC.

www.ingramcontent.com/pod-product-compliance
Lightning Source LLC
Chambersburg PA
CBHW022046080426

42734CB00009B/1262